This is Your Story

A book for young warriors
seeking Jesus

Kate French

Eremite Publishing
ISBN: 978-1-952139-19-2

Editor: Kelly French
Art Direction: Emily Speake
Interior Design: Kate French
Illustrations: Emily Speake, Winna, and Windha Sukmanindya

For Ava and Micah:
Warriors for Jesus

Table of Contents

Your Story   9

The Beauty of Jesus   17

Jesus is Fun   19

The Power of Jesus   23

Jesus is Giving   25

The Love of Jesus   27

Jesus is Your Best Friend   31

Prince of the World   37

Demons   41

Sin and Separation   45

The Battle Starts   53

Armor of God   57

Holy Spirit   63

Angels   67

Prayer   71

The Bible   75

Growing and Persisting   79

Your Heart   87

Joint Heirs   91

One with Jesus   95

The Coming Kingdom   97

How to use this book

Welcome to the wonderful world of meeting Jesus through stories. Did you know that you have a place in God's story? You have a role! In this book, you'll learn about your role, your heart, and how valuable you are to God's story.

This book is written with the idea that you'll read one section a day. Just read a little bit, think about it, pray about it, and ask Jesus what he wants you to learn.

At the beginning of each section, there is a song suggestion. You can listen to this song before you read to help you be ready for what you're going to read. You could listen to it after you read the section to help you think about what you read. Or you could not listen to it at all! That's okay, too.

At the end of the book is a section labeled Guided Reading. Here, you have more songs, videos, movies, TV shows, and questions to help you learn more about what you read in the book. It's not supposed to be homework – who wants more of that?! But if you feel you want something to help guide you as you read, feel free to dig into the Guided Reading.

More than anything, I hope this book helps bring you closer to Jesus, Papa God, and the Holy Spirit. They are my best friends, and I think they could be yours, too.

The Great Story

Your Story

"Gather Round, Ye Children, Come"
By Andrew Peterson

Adventure. Journey. Suspense. Riddles. Love. Battle. Mystery. Intrigue. Reunion. All good words, right? All good words because they make a story go from boring to exciting. They turn a normal day into an extraordinary day. Your imagination grows just by learning these words. I think they may even speak to your heart. They pull on the place in your heart that says, "Let's be more! Let's do more!" There's something in your heart that calls to you, inviting you into a greater story – into something greater than yourself. Movies and books and all sorts of stories speak to our hearts, too, because they always include some of these words. Sometimes, you may watch a movie and feel inspired, connected, and like you want to be in the movie, too! I know I have. There's a reason why movies can do this to you. Let's think of some famous stories, maybe some of your favorite stories, to see what I mean.

Moana is a brave girl who doesn't ignore the calling she feels in her spirit. She is called by the ocean to go out and find Maui to return the heart of Te Fiti. A big task. Along the way, the ocean helps her and guides her. The ocean leads her to Maui. The whole time she's traveling, she thinks

that she isn't worthy of the trip. She isn't sure why the ocean picked her. Then, it gets hard, and Maui leaves. Moana is left wondering, "Can I even do this?" She decides to give the heart back to the ocean and asks it to pick someone else. But Moana is reminded of who she is and who she belongs to. She is reminded that she's important and that she has value. She realizes that she can deliver the heart to Te Fiti. She - with the ocean - can do the job. So, she gathers her courage and starts out. But there is a terrible beast named Te Ka between her and Te Fiti. She has to fight and be clever and cunning in order to pass Te Ka. But she *is* clever, and it turns out she is never really alone. Maui comes back, and the ocean is there to help. When she makes it past Te Ka, what does she find? She finds that the monster is actually Te Fiti! Without her heart, Te Fiti has turned dark and angry. Without her heart, Te Fiti has become a tragic version of herself that disrupts more than just her. But what does Moana say? "This is not who you are. You know who you are."[1] Te Ka accepts her heart back and is restored to her original beauty. And she invites growth and beauty all around her. Each one - Moana, Maui, and Te Fiti - is restored to their first love by the end of the movie.

Superman is the good guy from a different world. He comes to Earth and loves the people and decides to save them. Several people try to stop him. Over and over he fights bad guys - Lex Luthor, The Toyman, Deadshot, and so many more. But he wins. He saves the people, he saves the world, and he defeats the bad guy. Sometimes, he is in great danger.

They are serious enemies. But Superman is far bigger and better. He never saves the earth for his own satisfaction. He doesn't save the earth so that he can dominate it and take it over. He does it because he loves the people of Earth and he wants them to love him, too.

Aladdin is down on his luck, but with a little help from the Genie, his life starts to turn around. Then, Jafar! He tries to kill Aladdin several times. After revealing who Aladdin actually is, Jafar dumps Aladdin into the sea. Another time, Jafar throws Aladdin away to a frozen tundra. But Aladdin doesn't stop; he doesn't give up. He comes back and saves Agrabah, Jasmine, and all his friends. The movie ends with Aladdin on top - as a real prince. From nothing to riches.

These stories might sound completely different from each other, but they aren't different at all! They each tell the story of great love coming and saving people. Love comes, reunites, and saves the people from the enemy or darkness that is trying to keep them separated. There's a reason all these stories go this way. It's because they're following another story that is so big, we can't ignore it. It's Jesus' story.

When God created the world, it was perfect. There was no evil. There was no distance between people and God. The people living in the world got to talk with God every day. They walked with him, shared stories with him, and enjoyed being together with him at any time. They weren't doomed to death; they were going to live forever. But then, Evil entered the story. He came to kill, steal, and destroy,[2] and he did it. The Enemy caused separation between people and God. He brought sin. God had

made a Perfect Place where people could live perfect lives and never die. Their hearts could forever belong to God. And because the people made a mistake and chose to agree with the enemy for two seconds, they couldn't live with God forever anymore. These people let sin enter the story, and with sin, they brought death – a complete separation from God. God knew that they would not be able to enjoy the Perfect Place in the same way anymore, and God's heart broke for his people. God knew that because there was sin, not only would his people die, but also the whole earth would start to die. It would fall apart. It was supposed to be perfect, like he created it. But it couldn't be perfect if it had sin in it. So, because God loved his people, he knew there was only one way to save them. He had them leave the Perfect Place. The Perfect Place wasn't where they belonged anymore.[3] It would be too tragic for them if they stayed.

But this isn't where the story ends! God doesn't say, "Goodbye, see you later." NO. Because of sin, there is now a battle to win back the human heart![4] For thousands of years, God has fought for his people. His beloved. He fought to bring them back to him. To restore the union they once had, so that humans would want their hearts to belong to God again. Then one day, he sent his son Jesus Christ, the Savior of all people, to the earth. Jesus came to Earth to defeat the Enemy once and for all, to win back the hearts of his people. And he did! He created a world where people can be reunited with God again. Where they can be connected with him. And

God said he was going to make a New Perfect Place! But we aren't in the New Perfect Place yet. We aren't in a place where we can physically walk with God. What's up with that? Well, the story isn't over yet. We're waiting for Jesus to come back again. And when he comes again, look out, World! Oh, I'm so excited for it!

The Glory Of Jesus

The Beauty of Jesus

"Most Beautiful" by Maverick City

Did you know that the human eye can tell the difference between ten million different colors? Ten million! If you tried to count to ten million, it would take you almost four months! That's so many! Do you know why you can see so many different colors? Beauty. When you are out in nature and look around, you're flooded with color and texture and lines and shades and beauty. Have you ever caught a glimpse of the sunset and been frozen from the beauty of the different colors on the horizon? Your eyes were made to catch different colors, and your brain was attracted to beauty because God created beauty as a reflection of himself.[5]

Think of the most beautiful thing you've ever seen. God's more beautiful.[6] One time, I was in the mountains, and there was fog coming in over the trees. The sun was starting to shine on the fog so that the whole valley started to glow. And I was blown away. One of my favorite beautiful things is singing. I love listening to really good singers because they're beautiful. Your heart is drawn to beautiful things because God is beautiful. Your soul wants to be with Papa God. Your spirit wants to know the Holy Spirit. Your heart wants to hang out with Jesus. Our whole body is drawn to beauty because Papa God, Jesus, and the Holy Spirit are the most beautiful thing in existence.

This is how we can connect with Jesus - by finding beauty. Beauty can

help restore your heart. What your friend thinks is beautiful might not be beautiful to you. So, go find it for you and let Jesus speak to you through it.

But beauty doesn't just mean good-looking. When we say God is beautiful, we don't just mean his face is pretty. When someone is playing basketball and they throw the ball perfectly through the hoop so the net swishes just as the buzzer calls the end of the game, someone in the crowd is saying, "beautiful."

In *Frozen 2* when Elsa is taming the water spirit, the waves are crashing, and it's terrifying, but she persists and finally tames the horse. This part of the movie has dark colors, and it can be scary, but it's beautiful how she uses her strength and power to take control over the situation.

Buddy the Elf from the movie *Elf* is walking home with his brother, and some mean kids come out and start throwing snowballs. Buddy doesn't run away or yell at the kids, he just makes a bunch of snowballs really fast and wins the snowball fight. It's beautiful how he connects, protects, and has fun with his brother. Then they spend the afternoon together finding a Christmas tree and just being friends. It's beautiful.

Jesus is beautiful in all of these ways. He's funny. He protects. He wants to connect with you. He's in the perfect moments. He's in the scary moments. He's the guy you want with you all the time, and this makes him beautiful. He can handle the good, bad, scary, and funny. He can handle everything. And the best part is, he'll always be there for you. It's so beautiful.

Jesus is Fun

"Crazy" by Newsboys

God loves to laugh. Can you imagine his laugh? Think about it for a minute. Imagine you said something really funny, and God heard it. He looks at you and his mouth starts to form a smile. Then, his smile reaches his eyes, and he starts to laugh. I bet his laugh is very deep and very loud, but lovely. You laugh together, practically falling over from the laughter. When you laugh, your heart feels lighter. God loves your heart and soul, so he gives you things to laugh about so you can feel free.

One of my favorite things to do is think about Jesus with his disciples – his twelve friends that followed him while he was on Earth. They were 13 men walking around the countryside going from town to town. They spent so much time walking and talking. I'm sure they had inside jokes – some things only they could laugh about. Somebody would do something funny, and then everyone else would laugh. Later they would remember and laugh again. Maybe they teased each other in good fun, like friends do. Jesus laughed. Because Jesus is funny.

Here's how I know: God created everything. He created humans to be like him. And humans love to laugh. We see things and we think they're

so funny that we can't help but laugh. If we are made to be like God, then God must laugh, too.

Have you ever seen a puppy? His feet are too big for his body, but he runs and jumps anyway. Sometimes, he runs and runs and can't stop. He can't stop, and the wall is getting closer and closer and BANG, he slides into the wall. He isn't hurt; he just shakes his head a little and gets back up to start running again. That's just fun. And sometimes very funny. And God made that puppy. God knows the puppy is funny. God knows you're funny. And he loves it.

One day, men were out fishing with big nets. They had been fishing all night long – all night long with their big nets and they had not caught one fish. They were at a lake that had lots of fish, but they didn't catch one. But these weren't just any men – they fished for their jobs. It was the thing they knew best. They knew where the fish liked to hide. They knew what the fish liked to eat. They knew the best time of day – or night – to catch fish. They knew where the best tasting fish lived. But they didn't catch anything. Well, morning came and still no fish. They were just having a bad fishing day. They decided to give up on fishing for the day. The fish were just gone. But then came Jesus. He was teaching on the shore and needed to use one of their boats so that everyone could hear him. When he got done teaching, he told one of the men, named Peter, to try fishing one more time. Peter agreed. When he dropped his net down, it filled up with so many fish that they didn't all fit in the boat!! They got a second boat to put fish in, and then both boats started to sink! So! Many! Fish! Jesus used a fun miracle to show these fishermen his power. But wait, there's more! Years later, Peter was one of Jesus' best friends, but Jesus wasn't with Peter in those days. Peter didn't even know where Jesus was. Peter was missing Jesus, and he was sad. So he went out fishing again. And just like the first time, he didn't catch any fish. But Jesus came again. This time he said, "Have you caught anything?" Peter didn't really know who was asking him this, but he said, "No." And Jesus said something really funny: "Why don't you put your net on the other side of the boat to catch some fish?" The other side? Jesus, fish don't only swim on one side of a boat! But Peter did it. And then just like the first time that Peter met Jesus, the boat started to fill up with so many fish that it started to sink! Aha! Peter knew now that he was talking to Jesus. Jesus used an old joke and made a new one to connect with Peter.[7] Can't you just imagine the laughter on Jesus' face when Peter came to shore? Peter probably said something like, "You *would* do that - 'fish on the other side!'" And Jesus

would say, "Hey, I thought it was a good idea," laughing with joy to be with his friends and to make jokes.

One time Jesus said, "It would be easier for a camel to go through an eye of a needle than for that thing to happen."[8] What? A camel is so big! How can it fit through the part of a needle that the thread goes through? Who even thinks of that? Jesus. Because he's funny. Another time, God was trying to get the attention of a man riding a donkey.

Three times he tried, but the man kept getting distracted. The man's donkey, however, noticed that God was trying to talk to the man. So after the third time, God gave the donkey the power to talk to the man so he would finally listen! A donkey that can talk?! So fun.[9]

God can be serious, yes. And God knows when to be serious. But God is our Papa, Jesus is our Brother, and the Holy Spirit is our Friend. Good papas, brothers, and friends are funny and love to have fun. And God is a good Papa.

The Power of Jesus

"Something About That Name"
by Sonicflood

A long, long time ago, there was Papa God, Jesus, and the Holy Spirit. But there was no Earth, no stars, no light, no people. Then, out of God's great power, he simply spoke, and things started appearing.[10] Imagine a king. He is sitting at his great table, and he says, "Bring me bread." And someone brings it. This king has power so that when he speaks, people act. But God's power is so great that when he spoke in the beginning, nature was created. Light was created. People were created. In fact, the whole reason God created the earth was so that people could live here. God wanted people to be like him, to love him, to be free, and to know him. When people first came, they walked with God every day, sharing life, stories, and love. So much power was used just so God could be close to his people and win their hearts.

Fast forward several years, and God's people are living in Egypt. But they aren't free. The Egyptians are keeping them as slaves making them work very hard without letting them worship God. God wants his people to be free. Because he loves his people and wants them to be close with him, he sends bugs and frogs and hail and blood and darkness to Egypt to try to convince the Egyptians to let his people go. He doesn't just send a little bit of bugs. He sends so many bugs that they couldn't see the ground anymore – only bugs! The Bible says that the darkness that God sent was the kind

you could feel and that people couldn't walk for three days because it was so dark they could not see anything! God tells the Egyptian leader to let his people go. Why? So they can worship God freely in the wilderness.[11] But the leader doesn't listen to God. So God keeps showing his great power. All because he wants his people to be able to come to him and worship him.

Fast forward hundreds of years, and Jesus is born. Jesus has some great friends that he loves very much named Lazarus, Mary, and Martha. One day, Jesus is told that his friend Lazarus is sick and is going to die. But Jesus doesn't go save him right away. He waits a couple days. When Jesus gets to the town where Lazarus lives, he knows that Lazarus is already dead. He sees Mary and Martha and sees how sad they are, and Jesus is filled with compassion and starts crying. He goes to where Lazarus is buried, he looks to Heaven, and he praises Papa God. Then he yells out, "LAZARUS, COME OUT!"[12] And Lazarus comes out! The power of Jesus is so great, all he has to do is speak, and nature reacts. Just like God when he created the world.

Think of the ocean. The waves can be very pretty. They can be calm. They can be fierce! They can destroy ships! They can make giant cliffs fall into the water. The ocean is so powerful humans can only swim so far into it by themselves before it's too dangerous and they have to come back. But who gave the ocean it's power? God did. Think of the strongest thing in the world. God is stronger! But God uses his power for one purpose. To bring you closer to him. He loves you so much that he focuses all his power and all his strength on becoming inseparable from you.

Jesus is Giving

"Psalm 46" by Jenny and Tyler

Do you remember the Cave of Wonders in the movie *Aladdin*? There are so many jewels and coins and gold and crowns and treasures down there. But Aladdin isn't allowed to touch any of it!

Have you ever tried to take a picture of a sunset? When you look at it with your eyes, there are so many different colors, and they all blend together so perfectly. A sunset or sunrise is one of the most beautiful things on Earth! But your picture just doesn't do it justice - the full beauty is missing.

Has your family ever made cookies? So many cookies, but then they tell you you can't have any. They smell so good and yummy, and they have the perfect amount of chocolate chips, but then your hand gets swatted, and the baker tells you to wait.

All these situations seem to have plenty to go around - there's a lot of treasure, there are a lot of colors, there are a lot of cookies - but you aren't allowed to have any of it.

That's not how Jesus works. He makes things, great things, and he says, "This is all yours. You can have it. You can have all of it." There aren't any tricks. There isn't a trap. He's serious. Jesus knows your heart and what

your heart longs for, so he gives you the things that are in your heart.

When God created the world, he filled it with animals and plants and fish and beauty. Then, he created Adam and Eve and he told them that they could have the WHOLE WORLD. That everything he had made was theirs to rule.

One time, Jesus went to a party, but the party ran out of everyone's favorite drink. So, Jesus made more of the drink. And he made it be more delicious than anyone had tasted it before, and he made way more than they were able to drink. He made the best, and he made the most. Because he loves to give. And he loves to give generously.[13]

One time, there was a man named Elijah. God loved Elijah very much. Elijah lived in a country that was suffering because there was no food and no water to grow more food. But God sent Elijah to live in a house that had just enough flour and oil to make one loaf of bread. Well, they were hungry, so they made the bread. But God cared for Elijah, the woman who owned the house, and her family. God told Elijah that he would feed him. Every day, they would wake up and find enough flour and oil to make one more loaf of bread. They never ran out.[14]

God gave to Adam, Eve, the wedding people, and Elijah. And God gives to you. God gives the best, and God gives the most. Why? Because he loves you.

The Love of Jesus

"How He Loves"
by David Crowder Band

Do you know what the best part of Jesus is? His great love. In fact, he's so great at loving, the Bible says that God IS love.[15] It doesn't mean that he's just really good at it. It means that everything about love comes from God. Without God, there is no love. Yikes. I'm glad there's God. See, everything that Jesus does is because he loves us. Can you imagine if everything you ever did showed that you loved someone? You would always be kind to your sister or brother. Every time your mom asked you to clean your room, you would do it right away! When you saw someone hurt, you would help them. And so much more. Maybe you already do those things. Good job. But the older you get, the harder it is to always show love. But Jesus was a grown man, and he ALWAYS showed love. There is never a time in the Bible when Jesus didn't show love. And Jesus did a lot of different things. He healed people. He taught people about Papa God. He taught them how Papa God wants to be close to them, just like people were close to God at the beginning of the world. He met people and understood what had happened in their lives, and he was able to comfort them. He was able to restore the hearts of the people. They were troubled because the Enemy had been fighting with mean tricks to

steal their hearts. But Jesus saw them and started healing their hearts. Jesus was the best guest at any party. He was the cool guy. If you were in a room with him, you would want to ask him a bunch of questions just to hear what he said. People loved to see him and hear him because they knew he loved them. But there is one thing that he did that proves without a shadow of a doubt that he loves us: He died so that we can live! He saw that all the people he loved would have to live hard lives and be far from God, and he wanted them to be able to be close to God. And he knew the only way to do that was to die for the sins of the people. To die for your sins. He took your place, and now you can be close to Papa God and Jesus.[16] Because the best part about this story is that Jesus didn't stay dead. He came back to life so that he could love you forever! You get to be happy in God's love forever.

This can be hard to understand, but there are a few stories that might help.

Remember in *The Little Mermaid* when Ariel agrees to the Sea Witch's contract? The Sea Witch says that if Ariel can't get Prince Eric to kiss her within three days, then she will become the Sea Witch's servant. But Ariel doesn't get Prince Eric to kiss her! She fails. Her father finds out about the deal. He finds out that Ariel is going to become the Witch's servant and decides to take her place so that Ariel can go free! He does this because he loves his daughter so much, he would rather take her punishment than have her be punished, even though it is all her fault.

In *The Lion, the Witch, and the Wardrobe*, two brothers and two sisters go into the magic land. They hear talk about a White Witch and a Great Lion. Everyone who lives in the land is afraid of both, but they love the Lion and hate the White Witch. But one brother, Edmund, decides that he likes the White Witch because she gave him candy and promised to give him part of her kingdom. So, he goes to find her and betrays his brother and sisters! As the story goes, the brother and sisters meet the Lion, and they love him. He is good. And they get to be with him, but they miss their brother. They are sad that Edmund went to the White Witch. And the Lion is sad about it, too. The brother and sisters love Edmund, but the Great Lion loves him more.

It turns out that the White Witch is only tricking Edmund! She isn't actually going to give him part of her kingdom; she just wants Edmund as a servant! But something worse happens. The Witch decides to use the old law that says because Edmund betrayed his people when he went to the White Witch, she gets to kill him. Edmund is going to die because of what he did. But he is very sorry and wants to go back to the Lion. The Lion loves Edmund so much that he decides to take Edmund's punishment. The Lion tells the Witch that he will die instead of Edmund. And guess what? She kills the Lion. And Edmund lives. And Edmund is able to join his family again. The good news is that the Lion doesn't stay dead. After a while, everyone is gone, and the Lion comes back, bigger and stronger and ready to defeat the White Witch once and for all.

The Lion didn't want to die, but he did want to save Edmund. He gave up

his life for his friend, for Edmund, so that he could have a full life.

That's what Jesus did for you. Because of his great love, he, like the Lion, let the Enemy kill him so that you could have a full life, a big life, a life that doesn't end and doesn't have a limit. A life full of greatness and, of course, Jesus.

Jesus is Your Best Friend

"What a Friend We Have in Jesus"
traditional hymn

Once there was a young girl who loved horses. She loved to ride them and brush them and just be around them. She loved how tall they were and how fast she could run with one. She loved that the horse was tender and gentle, but also strong and powerful. Sometimes, she would take her horse out into a field and just be with the horse for hours, imagining and thinking. Then, she met a little boy who loved animals, but he had never been around a horse before. They started playing together and the little girl introduced her horse to the little boy. And the little boy started to really like horses. He could see how powerful and cool they were. He loved all the stories that mentioned horses. He loved that they were used in the Pony Express – a mail system before there were cars that would take the mail from one side of the country to another super fast. Before long, the little girl and little boy were best friends. They played together, but they had a special bond because they both loved horses.[17]

What is your most favorite thing? Did you know that Jesus loves that, too? In fact, you like your most favorite thing because God liked it first. God is like the little girl who loved horses. When God met you, he started telling your heart about all the cool things he loves, and you started loving

them, too.[18]

You have a lot of things in common with God. Did you know you kind of look like him? And you're funny like him. You like to look at beautiful and cool things just like he does. You love people, and God loves people. God is the best friend you always wanted. You can tell him anything and everything. You can ask him for help, and he'll help you. He loves to spend time with you, doing whatever you're doing - playing outside, making up cool stories in your room, coloring, watching T.V., eating - anything! One time, Jesus was hanging out with some friends, and he told them that he was going to create a home for them, a New Perfect Place where we could all live together. A place where we could be with Jesus and never be separated. He said that wherever he is, he wants his friends to be there, too.[19] And until the New Perfect Place is finished, he was going to send a special part of himself called the Holy Spirit to come and live with us here on Earth so that we could always be close to Jesus.

Jesus will never leave you. Papa God will never call you mean names. The Holy Spirit will always be there to give you confidence and a Friend. God is the best friend you could ever ask for.

Prince of the World

"Praise God, Shame on the Devil,
Amen!" by John Martin Keith

All great stories have a villain. Superman has Lex Luthor. Snow White has the Evil Queen. Aslan has the White Witch. Your story is not any different. God's story is not any different. There is a villain, and he rules the world. He lurks, schemes, and searches the world for friends of God – including you. He does this so that he can steal their hearts and ultimately hurt God. But God's not afraid. He's confident. Let me tell you more of the Enemy's story, and maybe you'll see why God's not afraid.

A long time ago, when Papa God was with the Holy Spirit and with Jesus, but humans weren't made yet, there were angels and spirits that lived with God. They were so happy to be with God, because God is the best god. He's your best friend. He was their best friend, too. But one angel was not happy. His name was Lucifer, and Lucifer means "Son of the Morning." His name means that he was shining with a special kind of radiance.[20] Because he was special, he started to want more. He wanted to be better than God. He wanted to be the best, to be the most beautiful. But he could never. Time went on, Earth was made, and this Enemy thought of a plan. He would rebel against God and take humans away from Him. The people who followed the Enemy followed because they were deceived.

Tricked! And because the Enemy's heart was now bad and didn't love God anymore, God cursed him to stay on Earth – and he couldn't come back and live with God anymore.

People don't really call the Enemy Lucifer anymore. Some people call the Enemy the Prince of the World or the Prince of Darkness. Remember, this Enemy was once a spirit in God's kingdom. This means he has power and abilities humans don't have. But he can't live in God's kingdom anymore, so he uses his power and abilities to control the land he lives in – Earth. Since no one who lives on Earth is stronger than he is, the Enemy is called the Prince of the World.

The Enemy uses darkness and other rebellious spirits to trick people into hating God. The Enemy and his spirit-friends encourage people to be afraid. They encourage people to hate other people. They tell lies and trick people into believing them. They darken people's hearts. And worst of all, they encourage and trick people into running away from God.

Jesus once said this about the Enemy: "The thief comes to kill, steal, and destroy. But I have come so that you can have life, and have it to the full."[21] Jesus called the Enemy a thief because the Enemy goes against God any chance he gets with one main goal: stealing your heart away from God. Another time, Jesus called the Enemy the Father of All Lies.[22] This means that all the lies on Earth started with the Enemy. Those are terrible things the Enemy wants to do: kill, steal, destroy, and lie.

But what did Jesus do? He came to Earth so that you could have no end to your life, and so your heart can be restored to God. Your life can be like a cup overflowing with water.

Never ever has the Enemy ever even come close to defeating God. Sometimes, the Enemy is able to convince people or other spirits to do bad things, but he's never able to take a person away from God when that person wants to be with God. He's never able to make something dark if God and his people want it to be light. He's not even a big Enemy. He's a serious Enemy. But not a big one – not compared to God.

Demons

"God is Bigger than the Boogie Man"
from VeggieTales

Remember when we read that the Enemy has friends? It's true. When Lucifer rebelled against God, other spirits rebelled with him and came to Earth. And then again a second time, spirits rebelled. While they were in Heaven, they had to bow down to God, but they wanted someone to bow down to them. They saw that Earth was a place they didn't have to bow to God and could actually rule, so they came to try to take it over. The Enemy is the main bad guy, but, like the Kraang from Teenage Mutant Ninja Turtles,[23] there are lots of smaller bad guys who work for the Enemy. They have names like the Spirit of Death, the Spirit of Fear, and the Spirit of Hatred. Don't they have awful names? Well, they get named that because that is what their job is. The Spirit of Hatred has one job: to make people hate each other. The Spirit of Fear has one job: to scare people. The Spirit of Death has one job: to end things. Wouldn't that be an awful job? But these spirits like it. They like it, and they're good at it.

Remember the Enemy's big plan? He wants to make people run away from God and give their hearts to the Enemy. He'll do anything he can to get people to forget who God is. So, he hired all these spirits to help him with his goal. Most of the time, these spirits are like ninjas! They're

so good, people don't even see them working. They don't come and say to you, "Hello, I'm the Spirit of Fear, follow me." You would know it was a bad guy right away! You would say, "Get out of here! You aren't God!" Easy-peasy. These spirits have to be sneakier than that. Sometimes, they convince people you know to tell you something scary. Or, they cause accidents to happen. Or, the worst one, they tell you things in your own head. They whisper it to you so it sounds like you! While the Enemy and his demons can whisper lies to you and trick you into believing things that aren't true, they can't really get into your head. You and Jesus get to rule over your head, and it is a safe place.

Have you ever thought to yourself, "I really hate my sister right now!"? Or, "My friend needs to be punished!"?[24] Those are probably thoughts from the Enemy and his evil friends. They are telling you those things to steal your heart away from Jesus. They trick us into thinking their thoughts are our thoughts. But you don't actually hate your sister. And you don't really want your friends to be punished. You love your sister and your friends.

This might all sound scary, but let me tell you a good thing Jesus has done to stop these bad guys. The Enemy likes to use the dark to convince people that God's light isn't real. But Jesus is a light! And what happens when you turn on the lights? All darkness goes away! What happens if a room is really, really dark? It is hard to see anything in that room. But even a tiny little night-light can make it so you can see. A big dark room can be conquered with a small flashlight. You can use the flashlight to walk all over the room. Jesus is the light, and he gives all of us light to beat the dark. Jesus said, "This world will not be easy - you will have problems and will have to fight bad guys. But! Don't worry! I have defeated the Enemy and will help you, too!"[25] So, when we start to feel afraid, we can know that the Spirit of Fear is trying to scare us. But God has beaten the Spirit of Fear, and we don't have to be afraid any longer!

Sin and Separation

"Endless Night" from
The Lion King on Broadway

In a town called Awesome, there were two groups of people: the Abhorrers and the Rapporters. These people were very much the same except The Rapporters loved everyone and everything, and the Abhorrers hated everyone and everything. Everyone in this town was born an Abhorrer - full of hate. But as they grew up, they got to choose if they wanted to stay an Abhorrer or become a Rapporter - and become full of love. Once someone became a Rapporter, the Abhorrers would try to trick them to do mean things, to be hateful again. The Abhorrers thought it was funny. Sometimes, though, it worked. A Rapporter would be tricked into doing a hateful thing, and then he or she would feel sad and have to ask for forgiveness. He would be forgiven, of course, because Rapporters love beyond measure.

Now, both groups had a leader. The Abhorrors had the chief evil man who was hateful to his very core. The Rapporters had the best and greatest person in the whole town – the whole world, really – for he loved everyone more than anyone had loved them, and he never forgot to love. His name was Agape. All the Rapporters loved Agape and wanted to be more like him - to love better and better everyday.

Bobby was a Rapporter. He had made his decision when he was very young, and now at the age of 9, he was becoming more loving like Agape every day. But sometimes, accidents still happened.

One day, Bobby was playing on the ballfield with a group of young Rapporters. They were having a great time and didn't even notice when the Abhorrers showed up. The Abhorers said, "Hey, let's trick these kids into being mean and hateful! Won't that be fun!" One of the Abhorrers saw Bobby standing all alone. He went up to him and told him, "Those friends don't really like you, you know. You're standing alone here; why aren't you with someone?" (Really, they were playing baseball and Bobby was standing in the outfield! No one is supposed to stand with you in the outfield.) Well, Bobby thought about it. "Maybe they don't like me!" And he became sad. And his sadness made him angry. Bobby went back to the dugout. He was grumpy, so he didn't talk to any of his friends. Then, the Abhorrer came up behind him and said, "See, none of them are asking you what's wrong. They don't love you." Oh, Bobby thought about it, "They really don't! Well, if they don't love me, I'm not going to love them." One of Bobby's friends, who actually did love him very much, turned to Bobby with a smile on his face and said, "It's your turn to bat, Bobby." But Bobby looked at his friend's smile and only saw teasing, not love. And

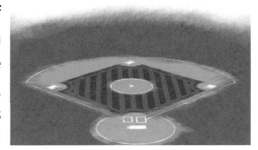

then Bobby, because he was angry and because he listened to the lie that the Abhorrer was telling, got up, kicked his friend, yelled at him, and ran home. As Bobby was running home, he passed Agape walking in the other direction. But Bobby was so angry, he didn't even see Agape strolling by. Agape had to call out three times before Bobby heard his name. "Bobby. Bobby. BOBBY!" Bobby stopped running and looked around. Agape was standing there with love in his eyes. He asked Bobby, "What's wrong?" Bobby told him all about how his friends were mean and didn't like him and just wanted to tease him. But Agape was wise. He had seen the Abhorrers walking to the baseball field, and he knew that the Abhorrers probably tricked Bobby. Agape looked at Bobby and said, "Bobby, I love you. You know I love you. And you know that your friends love you, too. I'm sad that you listened to the Abhorrers. What they said isn't true." Bobby, with tears in his eyes, said, "You're right. I'm sorry. I should go tell my friend I'm sorry, too." Bobby ran back to the ballfield and told his friend he was sorry. His friend told him, "I forgive you," and then they were able to finish the game.[26]

Who did the wrong thing here? Well, the Abhorrer tricked Bobby, and that was bad. But Bobby also did wrong. Bobby believed the lie that he knew was not true. And then, he grew hateful towards his friends. He became so hateful that he kicked one friend and yelled at him. And that was wrong. Bobby didn't kick his friend because he loved him. He kicked him because at that moment, he hated him. In that moment, the Enemy had won his heart. This is what the Bible calls "sin."

"Sin" is when we do something that isn't what God wants us to do. But we do it because our hearts are separated from God. The Enemy tries to trick us into sinning so that we stay separated from God. The Enemy shouldn't try to trick us - that's true. But we shouldn't be tricked into doing evil things. We are still responsible for the things we do. Especially when they hurt people.

God can't be around sin. So, if you have sin in your heart, you can't be around God. Yikes. The worst thing. Remember, God is the best friend anyone could have. I want to be with him all the time. But when we sin, we are separated from God. And that's exactly what the Enemy wants. He wants you to be separated from God. That's why he told you the lie in the first place. Sometimes, his lies are very good and very convincing. You are not alone, though; everyone has been tricked by him. Except one: Jesus. Jesus came to Earth, and the Enemy tried and tried and tried to trick him. He used every trick he had, but Jesus always remained united with God. He never believed any of the Enemy's lies. And that's why God sent Jesus to Earth, so that Jesus could help us stay united with God and to win back our hearts.

Fighting the Great Battle

The Battle Starts

"More than a Conqueror"
by Jasmine Tate

We have a Lover of our hearts. The Champion of our spirits. We have someone who is for good. Jesus. Papa God. Spirit.

And we have someone who rules in darkness. The Destroyer of hearts. Captor and tyrant of our spirits. Someone who is for evil. The Enemy. Prince of the world. Prince of darkness.

How can two polar opposites live in the same place? They cannot. When you try to shove two wrong sides of a magnet together, they push away from each other. Evil and good cannot live in the same heart. Sometimes evil comes in and takes over good. Or good comes and takes over evil. But they can't live in the same place.

But the Lord your God is good. He is faithful. He pursues you. He loves you. He forgives you. And so he fights for you. His great plan does not end with you struggling every day to be with him. No, no. His plan ends with you celebrating in his house with him. With no struggle. Free to be free. But how does freedom come? How does peace come? How does a never-ending, never-pausing, always-together relationship come? Someone had to fight evil.

You remember in *Star Wars: Episode VI - Return of the Jedi* when the Ewoks

and Han, Leia, and Chewie are fighting on Endor against the Walkers and Storm Troopers to get into the building to turn off the shield surrounding the new Death Star? And then in the sky, there's an epic battle going on between the Rebellion and the Empire. X-wings battling TIE fighters. The Millennial Falcon fighting the lead ship. It's action-packed, full of shooting. The good guys pull ahead, and then the bad guys take the lead. We lose people. They lose people. More people come to help us. But then they get more people, too. All this for one goal: the Rebellion (the good guys) wants to destroy the new Death Star so that they can save their homes and lives.

But that's not what Luke is doing. What is he doing? He's going after Darth Vader. By this point in the story, we know that Darth Vader is actually being controlled by Supreme Leader Palpatine. Darth Vader wasn't always a bad guy, in fact, he just might have a good heart. But Palpatine? He's no good. So, Luke goes on a mission to take out the Supreme Leader and save Darth Vader. What happens? The most beautiful thing. Luke finds Vader and helps him realize goodness. He saves him and brings him back to the light where he takes back his name of Anakin. And what happens to Palpatine? The evil man falls to his death. Victory belongs to Luke. But does everyone else know it? Does the fighting stop going on outside the ship and down on Endor? No. They keep fighting. The battle continues. The great evil leader of the Empire has fallen, but his minions keep fighting.

This story of Luke, Anakin, and Palpatine is similar to the story God is telling. As we've discussed, God's people were separated from him when sin entered the world. God can't be around sin, but all people had sinned![27] As you know, God wants to be connected with you, so he sent Jesus to die for you. But how does that work? Why does Jesus' death help you get connected with God again? Because Jesus took all the sin of the world, all the sin that everyone has ever done and all the sin that everyone would ever do - he took it all with him when he died. Remember, God is a big God, and he does not allow the Enemy to take away a person that wants to be with God. So, because of his great love, because he's your best friend, because of his power, because he is giving, Papa God sent Jesus to Earth to save the people – to save you. Instead of you dying because of your sin, Jesus died. Jesus took your place and gave the ultimate sacrifice so that you could be with God again - with your sins forgiven and your heart clean. And because Jesus died, you don't have to die. Sometimes, people's bodies still break and fail; bodies do die. But Jesus didn't die to save your body. He died to save your soul, spirit, and heart. Those things never die. One day, your body will probably fail and stop working, too. But you don't have to fear your body's end, because you are more than just a body.

Now, this is the great part. And this is where the action is. In his death, Jesus looked the Enemy in the face and laughed. Jesus knew that Papa God was better, greater, wiser, bigger, stronger, and lovelier than the Enemy would ever be. And God won. The Enemy was put to shame and lost against Jesus. Do you know how? Because Jesus did not stay dead! Jesus died with all of the sin of the world and the people attached to him.

And then he walked out of the grave clean of sin and totally free! The Enemy is lord over death, but Jesus walked out on death, defeating and conquering the Enemy. Huzzah! Thank you, Jesus. It's because of this that we can have salvation and that we, too, can live forever!

But just like when Luke and Anakin defeated Palpatine, the battle is not over. People are still fighting and will have to continue to fight until everyone finally knows that the battle is over and our winning side can celebrate!

Now, it is your turn. Your heart is being fought over, and fight you must! Fight the Enemy. Fight alongside Jesus. Fight until Jesus comes back. But you know what the Bible says? You are more than a conqueror[28] because Jesus already won the war. You can fight without fear because you know who wins – Jesus! You can fight against the Enemy's schemes and know that you will conquer. You can fight because the God who loves every part of you is fighting for you and fighting through you. The Enemy will never win because you are a part of God's family. He will attack, but you know a secret the Enemy cannot accept: He's done for. Victory is ours! Victory is Christ's! Victory belongs to God! Hallelujah!

Armor of God

"Build Your Kingdom Here"
by Rend Collective

When Mulan cuts her hair and decides to ride off to battle to take her dad's place in the war, what does she make sure she takes with her? Her father's armor and sword.

When Wonder Woman decides to leave her island to fight against evil, what does she take with her? Her armor, her sword, her shield, and her whip.

When Father Christmas comes to the children of Narnia, what does he give them? A sword, a bow and arrows, and healing medicine.

Weapons. Protection. Why didn't they go in their comfortable clothes? Why didn't Father Christmas give them a gaming system? That would have been cool! It's because they were going to battle. They had to fight. And they had to be prepared.

In the same way, God gives you ways to protect and defend yourself. One of God's friends, Paul, wrote down and explained the armor that God has given us.[29] He says we need to put on the armor of God so that we can fight against the Enemy and his tricks. Now, the armor of God isn't something that you can physically pick up. There isn't a secret hiding place somewhere, a secret cabinet, or a highly protected cave you have to find

in order to get the armor. But each piece of armor represents another gift God has given that you can use right now, today, to start fighting against the Enemy. We don't use these things to fight against other people. Paul says, and we know, that the real bad guy in life is the Enemy. He uses our friends, our family, other people, and the Earth to try and keep us separated from Jesus. So, when you put on this armor, remember who you are fighting against and who you are fighting alongside. God has won the battle, but the Enemy is not gone yet. Fight with God and against the Enemy. God says that above all else, we need to protect our hearts.[30] Our hearts are valuable. They are being fought over. The Enemy is trying to steal them away from us. So, we need to protect them.

Paul says that God's armor includes a belt, a breastplate, shoes, a helmet, a shield, and a sword. You have something to protect you all the way around. And, I bet you'll look cool when you wear it all. The belt is truth. When you believe truth, know truth, and live in truth, nothing can knock you down. You are tied up in protection from lies.

The breastplate is righteousness. And righteousness is like goodness. God gives us goodness, but you can also have goodness come out of you. You can do good and be good. But this is a gift from God to help you fight. So when we put on God's righteousness, we are able to know what Jesus would do and we're able to do it. Would he step right or left? Would he stay or go? Would he fight or walk away? Would he speak or be quiet?

Would he say this or that? God's righteousness lets us know and act more like Jesus. When you're faced with a situation, any situation, or you need to make a decision, you can say, "Jesus, what should I do? What would you do?" Then you listen for his answer – it is always good.

Shoes are peace. But not just any kind of peace. Paul says to put on shoes so that you can be ready. And you're only really ready to fight when you have peace in your heart. You can't be ready to fight when you're hateful. You can't be ready to fight when you're bitter. You are only really ready to fight when you know that God is in your heart. And when God is in your heart, you're already a winner. You've already won. And a great steadiness comes with that. You aren't afraid to fight because you already know that being with Jesus is better than anything else in the world. And this gives you peace.

The shield is your faith. Have you seen what people do with shields? Sometimes they use it as a weapon. They'll hit someone with it, knock them out of the way, and take out their opponent. But most of the time, a shield is used to protect yourself. If something is flying through the air, you can lift your shield to cover your face. You can crouch behind it to stop arrows, javelins, spears, and more! You can use it to protect yourself at a close range, like from a sword, but also at a great distance, like from an arrow. This is like your faith. When you believe in God, attacks can come from near or far. They can be all different kinds, but when your faith is strong, you can stand behind your faith, like you stand behind a shield, and nothing will reach you.

Your helmet represents your salvation. Salvation is a gift that comes

when you believe in Jesus. But what salvation means is that your spirit will live forever with God. Your heart, that was so easily tricked by the Enemy before, will start to be restored. You'll have a whole heart again – able to live for Jesus. Some people forget and think that when their body stops working and their brain stops sending signals that that is truly the end, that it's over. But that's not the end because you are not just a body with a mind. You are a soul and you have a spirit just like God has a Spirit. And your soul and spirit will never die. When you know that you have salvation, you no longer have to fear the Enemy because the Enemy can't take salvation away. He can take other things like friends, things, and treasures, but never your salvation. Having salvation means that you get to start living now and forever with Jesus. You don't have to fear death, because you know that even after your body dies, you're with Jesus.

And your sword! Mushu yells out to Mulan, "WAIT! You forgot your sword!"[31] You can't forget your sword, even Mushu knows that. You need a weapon to attack. So far, all the other gifts are protection, but a sword is really about action and fighting. The sword is God's Spirit. The Spirit of God is one with God, so it can fight stronger than anything else. In fact, the Spirit of God has already overcome the Enemy. The Spirit of God fought and won and will do it again and again to protect you. Here's a cool thing: the same power that raised Jesus Christ from the dead lives inside of you![32] When Jesus came to Earth and was raised from the dead, all authority was given back to him.[33] He is the most powerful thing on Earth, more powerful than the Enemy and the demons. Jesus said to the crazy waves, "Be still," and they calmed down.[34] God's Spirit, just like Jesus, has all the power, all the authority. When you have the Spirit of God living inside you, you can say to a problem that looks as big as a mountain, "In the name of Jesus, MOVE!" And it will have to leave you alone. The Spirit of God is the sharpest sword; the straightest arrow; the strongest battle-axe; the fastest bullet. And the more we learn from God about the Spirit, the more we recognize the Spirit in our lives.

All of these things together – truth, righteousness, peace, faith, salvation, and the Spirit – let you stand and fight. You will have to go into battle, and these pieces of armor and weapons will help. It will be hard. It might last a long time. You'll have to be courageous. But when the fighting is over, you'll still be standing there, side by side with Jesus.

Holy Spirit

"Holy Spirit"
by Bryan and Katie Torwalt

Papa God is a good, good Father. And Jesus is King. And the Holy Spirit is the giver of strength and life. Jesus walked on this world for many years and he had many friends during that time. When it was getting close to the time for him to die, he told his friends, "I'm going, but you should be glad that I'm going because when I leave, I'm going to send the Spirit in my place, and he'll be with you."[35] This can be hard to understand. We understand that Jesus died, fought the Enemy, won, came back to life, and then he went to be with Papa God so that he could prepare a home for us! Hallelujah! But if Jesus was gone, who was going to defend us? God sent another part of himself – his Spirit. His Spirit is very much God, just like Jesus is very much God. They all work together like a candle with three wicks. They are all the same candle, but they burn separately. In fact, the Bible describes the Spirit of God like fire and like wind – strong forces that people can't really explain, but we know they are there. The Holy Spirit can't really be seen, but he can be felt. And the Holy Spirit has come to be your comforter and your guide. He will lead you and instruct you.

When you decide to believe Jesus, oh, this beautiful thing starts to

happen. Your heart starts to transform and renew. It starts to heal and grow and restore. This all happens because the Holy Spirit comes to live with your spirit. You two become connected in a way so that nothing can separate you. Now, evil spirits will try. And sometimes it will be hard for you to feel the Holy Spirit, but he's with you, and he loves you.

One time when I was younger, I went to an apple orchard. There were hundreds of apple trees growing in straight lines with beautiful red, yellow, and green apples. So many beautiful shades of apples. The trees didn't have to work and think really hard to grow apples, they just did it because that's what kind of tree they are. And if it had been an orange tree, it would grow oranges. But an apple tree doesn't grow oranges. And an orange tree doesn't grow apples. When the Holy Spirit lives inside of you, you will grow fruit, too. You won't suddenly have apples coming out of your arms – that would be weird! But the fruit of the spirit is love, joy, peace, patience, kindness, goodness, faithfulness, gentleness and self-control.[36] When you have the Holy Spirit living inside of you, these things will come out of your heart easy peasy lemon squeezy. You won't have to fight, fight, fight to love your sister or brother or friend. It will become easy.

When the Holy Spirit is living inside of you, he can protect you from demons and the Enemy. When you are afraid, you can say, "Fear, go! Holy Spirit, come!" And Fear will have to go. He's afraid of God. You can use your armor of God and the power of the Holy Spirit to protect your room, your home, your body, your family, your favorite blanket. Your God fights for you through the Holy Spirit, and you can fight for yourself with the Holy Spirit. If you are having trouble sleeping, you can say, "Holy Spirit, help me sleep. Clean my room of any bad things and give me peace." If you feel afraid, you can say, "Holy Spirit, you are my King, and all other spirits have to leave! The Spirit of Fear has to go! Only the Holy Spirit has power here! In the name of Jesus!"

If you want the Holy Spirit to live in your heart, all you have to do is ask him to come live there. You can give it to him. But you can't just give him a little room in your heart; you have to give him your whole heart. "Holy Spirit, I give you my heart. Make it your home. All other demons have to leave because I only let the Holy Spirit live here. In the name of Jesus!"

Angels

"Rescue" by Lauren Daigle

You already know that we are not alone in the world. The Holy Spirit and evil spirits live here. And the Bible calls God the Elohim of elohim.[37] But what does that mean? Well, "elohim" is a Hebrew word that means spiritual beings – beings like the Holy Spirit and evil spirits that came from Heaven and lived with God before the world was created. So, God is the Elohim of elohim, meaning he's the top and the best, and it's only from him that we get life. But there are more elohim than just spirits and God. Angels are also elohim.

Angels live in the spiritual world, and they work for God. They worship him and love him, and therefore, they fight for him. And since you live for God, the angels fight for you, too.

There is a story in the Bible about a man named Daniel. Daniel had a vision about a great war that was going to happen, but he didn't understand the vision, so he asked God what it meant. But he didn't hear from God, so he started to pray every day. He prayed so much that he didn't eat any of his favorite foods or drink anything but water. He really wanted to understand what was happening – to understand the war and what God wanted. After 21 days of praying, Daniel saw what looked like a

man – except the man was shining! His face was like lightning and his eyes looked like fire. This was a serious thing. An angel had come to Daniel. Everyone who was with Daniel became afraid and went to hide, and Daniel was left alone with the angel. The Angel said to Daniel, "Don't be afraid." Then he told Daniel that 21 days ago when Daniel started praying, God sent this angel to come and tell Daniel about the war. But evil spirits who were controlling the land where Daniel lived had tried to stop this angel from entering. They were fighting for many days – the angel wanting to get to Daniel, and the evil spirit trying to stop him. Finally, an even more powerful angel came and helped Daniel's messenger get past the evil spirit to tell Daniel about the war.[38]

Isn't that crazy? That actually happened. In the world we live in. Angels go on missions for God. Sometimes, their mission is to fight the evil spirits that try to convince us to follow them. Sometimes, they deliver messages. Several times in the Bible, angels come to women and tell them that they are going to have a baby. Isn't that fun – wouldn't that surprise your mom if she had found out you were going to be born because an angel told her? That's special. That happened to Jesus' mother here on Earth. An angel came to her and said, "Don't be afraid. God sent me to tell you that you are going to have a baby!"[39]

Did you notice that when the angel came to Daniel, he told him, "Don't be afraid"? And when the angel came to Mary he also said, "Don't be afraid." Angels are intimidating. They have to be fierce warriors to fight the evil spirits. But we don't have to be afraid of them because they fight for us and with God.

   You can ask God to send angels to protect you and to help you. When you are feeling scared or attacked, you can ask God to send angels to surround you. My mom often prays for angels to come around our car so that we don't get hurt while we're inside it. You can do that, too. Angels will help you defeat the Enemy and the evil spirits.

Prayer

"What a Beautiful Name"
by Hillsong

The armor of God is full of great gifts from God to help you protect yourself. Prayer is another awesome tool God gave us to protect ourselves and be closer to Jesus. Prayer is mighty, and prayer is powerful. Prayer is what we call it when we talk to God. When you have a conversation with your Father in Heaven, with Jesus, with God's Spirit. You can tell him about your day – that's prayer. You can tell him about a kid who hurt your feelings – that's prayer. You can thank him for giving you something like food or salvation – that's prayer. You can ask him to help you – that's prayer. You can ask him if he loves you – that's prayer. But prayer isn't just *you* talking. Jesus will talk, too. Maybe you won't hear a response in your ears, but Jesus likes to let you know what he's thinking. Sometimes, you'll know it is him because you can feel it in your stomach or your heart or your brain. You have a thought and you just *know* that it is him. For example, you can ask him right now, "Do you love me?" And he'll answer, "Yes." Try it and see how you hear the "yes." Maybe it's in your head. Maybe you get goosebumps. Maybe your stomach feels tingly. All of those could be your "yes." But if you tried it and nothing happened, try again. Focus, get quiet, go to a quiet place, ask him, and then be still

and wait. It's a good idea to start with this question because we already know the answer. Jesus loves you! So, if you are listening, and you hear a "no," you know that that is NOT Jesus. But when you sense that "yes," you can know Jesus is talking to you. He's talked to me before, and I know he wants to talk to you, too.

Prayer is a powerful thing. You can use prayer to grow your relationship with Jesus. Did you know that when you were in your mama's belly, you started to learn her voice? Even when you were so small and you weren't even breathing air yet, you started to learn who your mama was. Then, when you came out and you met her, you already knew her voice. You knew it right away. You also knew who wasn't your mama because of how you felt when you were with your mama. That's how it can be with Jesus. You're still small, but as you listen and grow and ask Jesus more and more questions, you will start to learn his voice. You will learn what it feels like to be with him. You will know when you aren't near him because the voice and the feeling will go away. And the more you learn his voice and what it feels like to be around him, the more you'll recognize evil voices. The Enemy has a voice, too. He'll try to trick you, kill you, steal from you, and destroy you. But Jesus is the voice of full life![40] Listening to him in prayer and knowing the difference between the voice of Jesus and the voice of the Enemy helps you fight lies and follow truth.

Prayer is a weapon. Paul, God's friend, told us about the armor of God.

Right after he talked about the armor, he said that we should pray in the Spirit all the time, no matter what is happening. He says that we should pray about all the Lord's people and to be alert.[41] So, when Jesus died and rose again, he told his disciples that a Comforter was coming, and this Comforter was God's Spirit. He said the Holy Spirit was coming to everyone who believed in Jesus. And he lives inside of you, too! If you believe. God's Spirit is very powerful, and you can use God's Spirit – through prayer – to defeat demons and the Enemy. When you are afraid, you can say, "In the name of Jesus: Fear, go!" If you are feeling hateful, you can say, "By the power of the Spirit: Hatred, leave!" And they have to leave, because they cannot live where God lives. You have that power. Thanks, Jesus!

One time, Jesus' friends asked him how they should pray. Jesus told them, "Pray something like this: God, you are so, so good! Your name is so, so good! The best name in the whole world! Wow! God! I love you. God, on Earth, things sometimes happen that you don't want to happen; the Enemy is a bully. So I pray that he doesn't have power anymore. I pray that the things you want to happen do happen on Earth! Just like they do in the Perfect Place. Please, give me what I need for today and help me not focus on tomorrow. Forgive me for the bad things I did today – I didn't want to do them – I love you too much. And I want to forgive the people who were mean to me; help me forgive them. Jesus, I don't want to sin anymore; help me to stay away from sin, to fight the Enemy and keep him away so that you and I can be together forever. Because you are the best, your kingdom is the best, and I want you to have all the power and

all the glory forever and ever! Amen!"[42] See how much power is in that prayer? If you say that, or something like that, every day, you will grow closer to Jesus. You will be able to fight the Enemy. You will find a peace that no one will be able to understand. They'll walk by you and be like, "What makes that cool kid so unique?!" And you will know – it's Jesus in your heart.

The Bible

"Thy Word" by Amy Grant

Books are amazing things. They open up so many doors of imagination for us, don't they? Like, the books about Harry Potter. A story of a young boy who finds out he's the one destined to save the world from the most evil man ever to live. When we read the books, we get to know Harry's personality. We get to know what he looks like with his lightning-shaped scar and his round glasses and his continually messy hair. We learn stories about his life. We follow along his journey as he saves the world. And we learn this all from reading his books. And this is the reason people write books. Even boring books, like some of your school books. They were written so you can understand the topic. Your science book was written so you can learn about science. Your math book was written to help you practice math.

The Bible is a book – well actually several small books put together – written to help you get to know Papa God, Jesus, and the Holy Spirit. The Bible has a main character all throughout the book, and it's Jesus. Every story helps us know more about him and feel closer to him. Jesus doesn't actually come to Earth until almost the end of the book, but every story is getting you ready for his arrival. And then after he comes, the

stories are getting us ready for when he comes again! There are exciting things that happen in the Bible! In one story, a man fights people with the jawbone from a donkey![43] Yeah. And there are people who walk on water.[44] Crazy. There is a man who goes up on a mountain and asks to see God. God passes in front of him but only lets the man see his back. When the man comes down from the mountain, his face is SHINING! He has to put something over his face just so other people can look at him without hurting their eyes.[45] There are stories about great big feasts with lots and lots of food! There are stories about people having to escape in the middle of the night so that they don't get trapped. There's adventure! There's romance! There's mystery. There's magic. There's freedom! There are puzzles. Sometimes, people have crazy dreams about skinny cows and fat cows, and then other people come, and they just know what the fat cows represent.[46]

The Bible is a fun book to read. But the reason it's the best book to read is because God wrote it - for us. Remember how everything God does, he does so that he can be close to you, so that your heart can be healed? He just wants you to be near him and love him. So he wrote the Bible for you, so that when you read it, you can understand him better. Get to know him, and fall in love with him.

One time, Jesus was in the wilderness, and he was hungry! He didn't eat for forty days! Can you imagine? I'd be so hungry. But then, guess what happened. The Enemy came and tried to make Jesus worship him instead of worshipping God. He tried every way that he could. He tried to trick Jesus three times. But Jesus wasn't tricked. Not once. Do you know why? He had been reading God's Word his whole life, and he used it to grow a great relationship with God. And so when the Enemy tried to trick Jesus, Jesus was able to use what God said in the Bible to tell the Enemy to leave him alone! And the Enemy did.[47]

The Bible is a weapon. Some people call it a sword. And just like a sword, we have to be careful how we use it. Some people, who have been tricked by the Enemy, take the Bible and like to fight people that really just need to be loved. Other people, also tricked, like to take the Bible and use it to control other people, even though the Bible gives us freedom! And because they were tricked, a few people like to take the Bible and change what it says so that they can do what they want. But the Bible is truth. The Bible is God's Word. The Bible is used for love, growth, healing your heart, and union with Jesus. One verse in the Bible says that all of the Bible is told by God; we use the Bible to teach, rebuke, correct and train to help us become righteous and more like Jesus.[48]

Growing and Persisting

"Rest on Us" by Maverick City

Warriors. At this point, that's what you are. You are fighting, and you are loving, and you have the Holy Spirit, and you've learned how to pray. You are a warrior for Jesus. You have an important role in the story God is telling. You get to have joy and peace in Him. You get to be with your best friend forever and ever. You get to know the one true God who made you and loves you and knows everything about you. Wow!! I'm so happy. And guess what, there's more. That's right; there's MORE! I want to scream for happiness like Oh does in the movie *Home*. "My hands are in the air, and I just do not care!"[49]

God did not give you an important role so that you could be separated from him. Oh no. He gave you an important role so that you could get closer and closer to him. And that's the sweetest thing on Earth, or on any planet, really! Who wouldn't want to be with the one who invented all good things? Who wouldn't want to sit side by side with the best Storyteller ever? Who wouldn't want to live in a place that is so grand and fabulous, they use gold to make streets? I know I want to. But the closer you get to Jesus, the harder the Enemy will try to get you away. If you're climbing a mountain, it doesn't get easier at the top; it gets harder. But once you've

reached the top, oh, it's so worth it. So, you have to persist. You have to keep going. You have to fight harder. And the gifts God has given you will only grow as you grow.

And you can grow in the Holy Spirit. If you wanted to run a marathon, you couldn't run the whole thing on the same day that you decided to do it. Maybe you could run one mile, two miles or even six miles. But a marathon is 26.2 miles! People who want to run a marathon take time to prepare. They practice for weeks. Every day, they run, they stretch, and they get stronger. Some days, they work on speed and running fast. Other days, they work on being consistent. Some days, they practice running a long distance and gaining endurance. This is what it is like to grow in God's Spirit. He came to you, and he entered your heart. And maybe you started seeing fruit right away! Praise Jesus! But there's more fruit and more gifts that come with the Holy Spirit. You can have them. You can be blessed by them. You can grow in the Holy Spirit and get stronger, consistent, and greater in endurance. When you started, you were a young tree, a sapling. Maybe you grew five fruits. But how many fruits does a big, well-rooted, old tree grow? You can't even count them all! One time, my grandpa took a big ladder up to a pear tree. This ladder got 40 feet tall. He extended the ladder all the way, laid it against the tree, and had me climb up it to pick the fruit of the pear tree. I was so high up. We didn't hardly move the ladder, and I collected many bucketfuls of pears. Enough for hundreds of desserts and jars of jam. All from one tree. You can be like that pear tree. Your fruit can be so plentiful that we can't count it. You can grow up in the Holy Spirit and learn what he would do, how he would feel, and what he would say.

Prayer is a gift that grows. The more mature you are, the more you learn about prayer. One thing I learned is that Jesus likes to share his power. And he gave you access to prayer so that you could share his power. One time, there was a man named Elijah. God told him that he needed to pray to stop the sky from raining. So, Elijah did. And it didn't rain for many many years. Then, one day, God told Elijah that he needed to pray and ask for rain. So, Elijah did. He went up to a mountain, and he prayed very hard for rain to come. Then, he looked at the sky, and there was no rain, no clouds, nothing. What? Didn't God tell him to pray so that it would rain? But Elijah persisted, and he prayed again. Still no clouds. He prayed and prayed and prayed. Each time, there were no clouds, no rain, nothing. He prayed a fifth and sixth time. He wasn't just saying, "God, let it rain." No, he was praying long and with power and authority. He was praying so hard, and still nothing was happening. Then, the seventh time he prayed, his helper went and looked at the sky and said, "Elijah, there's a cloud as big as my fist." And Elijah knew that it was going to rain. So he left his praying place and went to prepare for the rain. God told Elijah to pray for rain, but it took Elijah seven times before the rain actually came.[50]

We don't know why it took Elijah seven times to pray for something that God told him was going to happen. But imagine what would have

happened if Elijah gave up after the first time he prayed and nothing happened. Would it still have rained? We don't know. But Elijah didn't stop. He persisted. He wanted to grow closer to God, so he continued to pray. Imagine how close Elijah must have felt to God when God spoke to Elijah and shared his plan and told Elijah that Elijah had a vital role in it. You can have that, too.

We've talked about how God will answer you when you pray, but he will also talk to you, first. Several times in the Bible, God calls out the name of someone when they weren't expecting it. But when we know the voice of God, when we talk to him every day, we'll be ready when this happens. You can grow in prayer and grow in knowing God's voice and be ready when he talks to you first.

One time long ago, a boy named Samuel lived in a place where people worshiped God. He lived there with a man named Eli. Eli worked for God, but it had been a while since Eli or anyone else had heard God speak. One night, while everyone was sleeping, Samuel heard his name being called out. He thought it was Eli, so he ran to Eli and said, "Yes. I'm here. What do you need?" But Eli said, "I didn't call you." It happened again and again. The third time, Eli realized that *God* was calling Samuel. He told Samuel, "Go back to bed, and if you hear your name again, say, 'Speak, Lord, your servant is listening.'" So, Samuel went back and laid down. And he heard his name, "Samuel! Samuel!" He looked up and saw a form of God there.

He said, "Speak, your servant is listening."[51] Samuel was just a boy, but God came to talk to him. And Samuel wanted to hear what he had to say. You can do the same. God wants to talk to you. You can communicate with the Holy Spirit. You can learn more from him than any teacher you've ever known. And you can invite him to talk by saying, "Speak, Lord, your servant is listening." And then listen.

The Hope Of Jesus

Your Heart

"Holiness" by Sonicflood

This fighting, it won't last forever. Just like in any story, there's an end to the fighting, and the villain is finally overcome once and for all. And then what happens? There's a party. A great big party with lots of food and dancing and fun and laughter and rejoicing. There's hugging and playing and reliving old memories, and wonderful, wonderful love just oozing out of everyone. They can't help it!

That's what's in store for you! Jesus came to save your heart, heal your heart, and restore your heart. Remember, this isn't the physical heart that is inside of you. Jesus cares about that heart, of course. But what we're talking about is who you really are, the part of you that lives forever... your soul... your heart. Jesus came to restore your heart and to make it one with his heart. He came so that the worries and burdens your heart carries can be given to him. Jesus came so that you can have life and have it to the full. So, starting now, you can rejoice in him. You can praise him with all you have. You can give him everything and start to feel carefree.

Your heart is the most valuable thing you have, and Jesus cares for it like no other. He wants to protect it and nourish it. He wants your heart to be healthy and clean and pumping really strong. You get to give your

heart to Jesus and make those things happen. You can invite the Holy Spirit to live in your heart so you can know him. You can ask God to heal your heart and make it new. When sin entered the world, your heart became broken and hard like stone. A man in the Bible named David wrote several poems to God. He asked God to clean his heart, make it new, and make it soft.[52] He wanted to be a man who listened to God above all else. And God did it. God healed David's heart.

The Bible says that people can become tired and it says that even kids can stumble and fall. But! For the people who hope in Jesus, he will give them new strength. They will walk and not become tired. They will run and not have to stop. They will soar on wings like eagles![53] This means that Jesus sees your heart, and he will keep giving you strength to fight the battle and win the battle so that you can be with him forever.

Your heart makes you special. And you get to control what lives in your heart. In fact, you are the king or queen over your heart. It's like your heart is a kingdom, and you get to rule it. You get to decide how to rule your kingdom. Since you love Jesus, the best way to rule your heart is to give your kingdom to Jesus and let him rule.

See, God takes care of you. Jesus once told the story of a shepherd watching his sheep. He said that when one sheep wanders off, the shepherd goes and finds it and brings it back to the rest of the sheep. He hunts it down and protects it from evil. He guards it and loves it. You are the sheep, and Jesus is the shepherd. When you are lost, he will come find you. When you wander off, he'll come after you. When you face evil, he will protect you. All you have to do is give him your heart. And make sure that you give your heart only to him.

 All this can start right now. Jesus is coming to heal your heart and to heal it forever. You get to be united with him forever. You get to rejoice in his glory forever! You get to learn from him and be more like him forever! And forever starts now! You don't have to wait until Jesus comes back again for forever to start. A prayer: "Jesus, come into my heart right now. I give it to you. You can rule my kingdom."

Joint Heirs

"The Family of God"
by The Gaither Vocal Band

I come from a small town. In this small town, we have a hardware store. This hardware store is really cool. They have tools, paint, small gifts - lots of things. Because it is in a small town, instead of paying them money right away, they will write down what you took and bill you later. My dad has an account there so that he can walk in, show the guy he took a shovel, and just walk out. Later, my dad will get a bill in the mail, and then he sends money to the hardware store. Here's the best part. This man at the hardware store knows that my dad is my dad. So, when I want, I can go into the hardware store, take some paint, show the man, and then the man sends my dad a bill. The man knows and trusts that my dad gave me the power to go to the store and take things in his name. I have the same power my dad does at the hardware store, just by using my dad's name.

Jesus, when he's on Earth, does the same thing with God in Heaven that I do with my dad and the hardware store. He walks around and says that he is the Son of God. All the people know that this means he is saying he has the same power as Papa God. Just like I can go to the hardware store and get some paint, Jesus can use his Father's power to heal, clean, or

forgive sins.[54] Isn't that cool?

Here's something cooler. The Bible says that we are brothers and sisters with Jesus.[55] Do you know what that means?! Papa God is also OUR Father! Jesus uses his power to heal, clean, and forgive. *We* can use his power to heal, clean, and forgive! The same power that brought Jesus back from being dead is inside of you![56] When God is your Father, you can ask the angels to protect you – and they will. You can tell the demons to leave you alone – and they will! You can demand that your house be cleaned of evil, the Enemy, and mean spirits – and it will be clean! You get to be a part of God's kingdom and enjoy all the glory that he has![57]

This is such great news. We talked a lot about how there is a fight to save your heart. But being a brother or sister to Jesus means that you have all the power you need to fight because Jesus already defeated them.

And if you can heal, clean and forgive things and others, it means you can heal, clean, and forgive yourself– not by yourself, of course, but with the power that God gives you by being his son or daughter. God forgave you for all your sins when Jesus died on the cross. But sometimes, we hold on to our sins and want to punish ourselves. But you can let them go. Let go of your sins and forgive yourself. And you can heal your heart.

Jesus says that he went to Heaven to prepare a place for us so that when we come, we can sit with him and Papa God and rule like kings and queens.[58] When you accept your place as king or queen, you now have a choice to make. Rule it yourself, or give it back to God. If you let God be the main ruler over your kingdom, you can be sure that God's power and righteousness is there. And, because now you're a king or queen in God's kingdom, you don't have to wait until you're in heaven to start using God's power. You see, your kingdom is some far off land that you have to imagine. No, are the king or queen over your room, your bed, your body, and the places you go – like school, grandma's house, and a nearby park. You can use God's power to control those places and things. As you grow up, your kingdom will get bigger. Maybe you'll get a car, a house, a farm! Maybe you'll get a business, a family of your own, or maybe you'll become President and have lots of people looking up to you. You can rule your kingdom with God as your power and strength. You can choose, today, to give your kingdom back to Jesus and let his power rule. That's what Jesus did, and you can do it, too.

One with Jesus

"I Don't Need Anything but You"
from Annie

One time, Jesus was praying. He told Papa God that he wanted his friends to be one with him. He said, "Like you and I are one, God, let them be one with us."[59] We've talked about how Papa God, Jesus, and the Holy Spirit can be physically separated from each other, but they are ultimately the same being. Jesus is saying that he wants his friends to be included in that. He wants everyone who loves him to be connected with him and with Papa God. Wow. And since he died so that your soul and spirit can live forever with him, you get to be a part of that gift, you are one of Jesus' friends who gets to be connected with him and Papa God and the Holy Spirit. Right now if you want. You don't have to wait until your body dies to start being one; you get to start right now. Wow!

Jesus described his relationship with us like a plant. There are many different leaves and flowers on a plant, but they all come from the same stem. Especially if the plant is a vine. Jesus says that he is the vine, and we are the branches. We grow out of him, but we're a part of him. If you break the branch off, then it will die. And if we don't have Jesus, we will die, too. But you get to be a part of the vine.[60] Hallelujah!

Do you remember the movie *Annie* when it is almost over, and Annie and Daddy Warbucks are singing together? Annie had been an orphan - alone - with no parents to take care of her, no sisters or brothers, and the lady at the orphanage is mean to her. She doesn't have anyone, but what happens? Daddy Warbucks finds Annie and brings her into his home. He falls in love

with her, and he loves her as much as a daddy ever could. He cherishes her and wants to give her everything. He decides not only to let her stay in his home, but to let her become a part of his family. He brings her in as his own daughter. This is what Jesus does for you. You get to be a part of his family, and that means you get to be with him forever. So, in *Annie*, bad people come and try to take Annie away from Daddy Warbucks. But he fights, and he searches, and he doesn't let her go. He goes after her and saves her from the evil. And when they're together again, they are happy and blissful. There's a huge party, and they celebrate that they're together now and forever. At one point, they sing, "Together at last. Together forever. We're tying a knot they never can sever. I don't need sunshine now to turn my sky to blue. I don't need anything but you."[61] That's you and Jesus. When this world is ended and you and Jesus don't have to fight the Enemy, you will rejoice together because you don't need anything but him and you have him! Ha'tchcha!

See, God isn't a far away God that you can't feel. He's here, and you can talk with him, you can rejoice with him, you can feel him. You don't have to write him a letter hoping that he'll read it. He is with you, and he loves you. Right next to you, in your heart, with your spirit.

A prayer: "Jesus, we love you. We love you so much. Thank you for being with us, for loving us, for forgiving us, for letting us be one with you. Jesus, you are so, so good. I bless your name. I accept my role in your kingdom. I give you my heart, soul, and spirit. My body, mind, and strength. I love you with all I am and give you all I have. I want to be one with you – I receive this gift."

The Coming Kingdom

"Goodbye World, Goodbye" by
W.J.J.M. Radio Gospel Quartet

In the beginning, when God made the world, he made the place where humans and God could walk together, a Perfect Place. Then, when sin and the Enemy entered, the humans had to leave the Perfect Place. But what has been God's goal since then? To become reunited with his people. He started by reuniting our hearts and souls to him. But there is coming a time when he will restore the Perfect Place, and we'll be able to live there again![62] That means no sin and no evil to distract us, to deter us, to displace us! Only Papa God, Jesus, the Holy Spirit, God's people, and goodness. Oh, what goodness.

When this happens, there's going to be a HUGE celebration! There will be a great parade! Have you ever been to a parade? There's music and dancing and laughter and so many friends together. In the parade are people and things you've been waiting for, wanting to see. And now, it's here! Jesus will be in the parade. And angels! The people from our stories, like Daniel, Elijah, Adam, Eve, Paul, and so many more! Loud trumpets and probably drums will sound and play as they walk by you. You'll be in the crowd, and you'll see so many people that you love there, too! All restored with joy deep in their soul.[63]

The beginning of the movie *Tangled* shows that Rapunzel is with her family just like she is supposed to be. Then, evil enters the story and tears

her away from her rightful place as princess. She lives most of her life thinking that she is supposed to follow the evil that took her, not realizing that it is evil. Then, on her birthday, she is filled with a dream to finally see the floating lights in person and not just from her window so far away. So, she gets her frying pan and goes after it. She fights for it. And she gets it. But when she finally sees the floating lights up close (lanterns), she realizes that her heart is longing for a new dream, that she is longing to be restored to what she was meant to be – what she was made to be. She was born the daughter of the king, but she was living like a servant! We meet a bunch of men in a tavern in the middle of the story and they all tell us about their dreams. One wants to be a concert pianist. Another wants to find love even though he's kinda ugly. Another wants to knit, and still another wants to sew. Flynn tells them about his dream of living on an island all alone. Flynn has been helping Rapunzel get to the lanterns, and along the way, he realizes that his dream has changed. What his heart wants is to be made whole. As the movie comes to an end and Rapunzel is finally reunited with her father and mother, there's a huge party! Flynn says that it lasts for a week! And everyone gets their dreams. The guy who dreamt of playing the piano goes on to be a world-famous pianist. The ugly guy finds love. And Rapunzel and Flynn are restored with new whole hearts. All their dreams, their deep longings, come true at the end of the story when they're finally all reunited and Rapunzel is restored to her rightful place with the king.

This is just like us. God created us to be with him, but then evil forced us to leave. But Jesus gave us desires in our hearts, things that made us search for him. He invited us closer and closer until we found him. Just like Rapunzel who started out wanting to see the lanterns, but then was led slowly to what her heart really longed for. She started out with a small dream, really, and it slowly grew to what her heart really wanted. Along the way, we met Flynn and that helped steer her journey. That journey made her realize she was the lost princess. And helped heal her heart. She didn't find Jesus along the way because this is just a story. But like Rapunzel, your dreams and desires are leading you to something bigger. Your story is about Jesus loving you and leading you to him. You have a journey with dreams that get bigger as you go along. They lead you to Jesus and your truest desire, a healed heart – a heart reunited with God.

And one day, when the fighting is over and we're finally reunited with God, like we're supposed to be, we're going to have a huge party! It's going to last for days! What's your favorite food? It'll be at the party! What's your absolute favorite good thing on Earth? It'll be there, too. All the things you lost that your heart aches for, you'll get them all back. And Jesus will be there. Papa God will be there. The Holy Spirit will be there. So many people that you love. God says that he is going to make all things new.[64] That doesn't mean he is going to make new things. It means that the old things we used to have, loved, but then lost, will be restored to us. Given back to us. What's something good you lost and really, really loved? That will be in God's New Perfect Place. And what's something God put in your heart? What's your dream? You'll see that come true in the New Perfect Place if you don't see it here on Earth first. God loves

you, and he's preparing a New Perfect Place for you to come and live in forever. There is going to be so much good there. Your heart, soul, a new body, your mind, your memories, your story will be whole and complete in God's glory. You will get to spend as much time with Jesus as you want, asking him questions, hearing his stories, working on projects together. He can tell you about all the things he loves about you, all the memories he has with you. Maybe you two can go fishing. You'll get to relax. And you'll get to have fun. There won't be sad crying because it's the Perfect Place. And you know what else? I don't think you'll ever get bored.

References

[1] *Moana*, 2016.

[2] John 10:10

[3] *The Jesus Storybook Bible.*

[4] Ezekiel 36:25-28

[5] Genesis 1:31, Psalm 139:13-14

[6] Isaiah 33:17, Psalm 50:2

[7] Luke 5, John 21

[8] Matthew 19:24 paraphrased

[9] Numbers 22

[10] Genesis 1

[11] Exodus 7-12

[12] John 11:1-44

[13] John 2:1-11

[14] 1 Kings 17:7-16

[15] 1 John 4:8

[16] John 3:16

[17] Made up by Kate and Jesus

[18] Psalm 37:4

[19] John 14:3

[20] *Captivating*, Ch. 5, Ez. 28:12-15.

[21] John 10:10

[22] John 8:44

[23] Nickelodeon TV show, https://nickelodeon.fandom.com/wiki/Kraang

[24] *Lilo and Stitch*, 2002.

[25] John 16:33 paraphrased

[26] Made up by Kate and Jesus

[27] Roman 3:23

[28] Romans 8:37

[29] Ephesians 6:10-17

[30] Proverbs 4:23

[31] *Mulan*, 1998.

[32] Roman 6:10

[33] Matthew 28:18

[34] Mark 4:39

[35] John 14

[36] Galatians 5:22-23

[37] Exodus 8:10, Video: Elohim from The Bible Project, https://www.youtube.com/watch?v=U5iyUik97Lg

[38] Daniel 10

[39] Luke 1:30

[40] John 10

[41] Ephesians 6:18

[42] Matthew 6:9-13 paraphrased

[43] Judges 15:13-16

[44] Matthew 14:22-32

[45] Exodus 34:29-35

[46] Genesis 41

[47] Matthew 4:1-11

[48] 2 Tim 3:16

[49] *Home*, 2015.

[50] 1 Kings 18

[51] 1 Samuel 3

[52] Psalm 51:10, Psalm 19:14, Psalm 119:11

[53] Isaiah 40:30-31

[54] John 5: 17-18

[55] Romans 8:17

[56] Romans 6:10

[57] Romans 8:17

[58] John 14:3, John 17:21

[59] John 17:41

[60] John 15

[61] *Annie*, 1982.

[62] John 14:3

[63] Revelation 21:5

[64] Revelation 21:5

Guided Reading:

This section is two fold. One intention is to help older readers guide younger readers through the material. There are questions, songs, movies, and other book suggestions that you can experience together and discuss what you read. They are to guide you into a discussion to help your young reader understand their role in the great story better. This is not intended to be used as homework. It is not a tool to make kids have extra work while reading; we want them to enjoy the reading.

The second intention is to provide resources to help older readers really delve into these topics. Some book suggestions might be too heavy for younger readers, but are perfect for someone interested in learning more about their role and importance in God's story. These books will be marked with an *.

General good reading and watching for kids or adults:

Movies: *What's in the Bible with Buck Denver*
          Original VeggieTales by Phil Vischar
          Star Wars
          Wonder Woman
          Psalty movies (especially Singsational Servants)
          Moana
          Tangled
TV: *The Chosen*
          Lois and Clark the New Adventures of Superman
Books: Elsie Dinsmore books by Martha Finley
          Chronicles of Narnia by C.S. Lewis
          The Jesus Storybook Bible by Sally Lloyd-Jones

The Great Story:
Song: "Gather Round, Ye Children, Come" by Andrew Peterson
Song: "This is not who you are" from Moana
Song: "All is For Your Glory" by Cory Asbury
Book: *Epic* by John Eldgredge*

Questions:
What does it mean to be restored?
Do you feel like God is taking care of you?
What are some ways you're in God's story?

Beauty of Jesus:
Song: "Most Beautiful" by Maverick City Music
Book: *Beautiful Outlaw* by John Eldredge*

Questions:
Is there a place where you find rest? What is restful about it?
What do you think is beautiful?
What is it about beauty that is so restful?
Read Acts 17:27. Why do you think God made beautiful things?

Jesus is Fun:
Song: "Crazy" by Newsboys
Song: "Shackles" by Mary Mary
Movie: VeggieTales - the original ones
Book: *Beautiful Outlaw* by John Eldredge*

Questions:
What's something you find really funny?
Has Jesus ever done something in your life that made you laugh?
Have you thought of Jesus as being playful?
Think about Jesus with his friends. Are you excited that he wants you as a friend, too?

Power of Jesus:
Song: "Something About That Name" by Sonicflood
Book: *The Jesus Storybook Bible* by Sally Lloyd-Jones

Questions:
Are Papa God, Jesus, and the Holy Spirit the same being?
Do you think you could handle the power Jesus has?
Why did God send weird things to Egypt? Will he send weird things to you?
Do you think that your words have power like God's words have power?

Jesus is Giving:
Song: "Psalm 46" by Jenny and Tyler
Book: *Beautiful Outlaw* by John Eldredge*

Questions:
What is your favorite thing on Earth?
Do you think Jesus gave that to you?
What does it mean to be selfish?
Do you think God is selfish?

Love of Jesus:
Song: "How He Loves" by David Crowder Band
Song: "Good Good Father" by Cory Asbury
Book: "Gospel of John"

Questions:
Who is the Holy Spirit?
Have you ever asked Jesus if he loves you?
What did he say? Maybe you can ask him now.
What does it mean to love your neighbor as yourself?

Jesus is your best friend:
Song: "What a Friend We Have in Jesus," traditional hymn
Song: "Jesus Will Still be There" by Point of Grace

Questions:
Have you ever felt lonely?
Did you know that Jesus was often lonely on Earth, even though he was surrounded by people? He didn't feel like his friends understood him. Do you feel understood?
Jesus came to Earth so that people could know that whatever they were going through, Jesus had gone through it, too. Do you feel like Jesus understands you?
How does it feel to have a Best Friend that will never ever leave you?

Prince of the World:
Song: "Praise God, Shame on the Devil, Amen!" by John Martin Keith
Song: "Run Devil Run" by Crowder

Questions:
Do you think God still loves the Enemy even though he left God?
The Enemy has power here on Earth, but you don't have to let him use his power on you. What's something you can do to stop his power?
If God is bigger than the Enemy, why is the Enemy so evil?

Demons:

Song: "God is bigger than the Boogie Man" from VeggieTales
Movie: *Where's God when I'm S-s-s Scared?* from VeggieTales

Questions:
Have you ever felt tricked into doing something you didn't want to do? How did that make you feel?
How do you feel knowing demons try to trick you into hating Jesus?
How is Jesus talking to you different from demons talking to you?

Sin and Separation:

Song: "Endless Night" from The Lion King on Broadway
Song: "Gravity" by John Mayer*

Questions:
Where is your soul?
Have you ever gotten upset and acted like Bobby?
Jesus loves you. Let's try telling him you love him and you're sorry for doing things that he doesn't like.

The Battle Starts:
Song: "More than a Conqueror" by Jasmine Tate
Song: "The Battle Belongs to the Lord," traditional hymn
Song: "Oh Holy Night" by David Phelps

Questions:
What does it mean that Jesus walked out on death?
Do you see a battle around you? Do you feel a battle inside of you? What does it mean to battle?
Are you fighting alone?
Why is the light better than the dark?
Even though our bodies will die, we should still take care of them. Why do you think that is?

Armor of God:
Song: "Build Your Kingdom Here" by Rend Collective
Movie: *Wonder Woman*, 2017

Questions:
How can you use your shield of faith in real life?
What is a way you can use peace against the Enemy?
Why can we trust in our salvation?

Holy Spirit:

Song: "Holy Spirit" by Bryan and Katie Torwalt

Video: "Holy Spirit" from The Bible Project*

Questions:

How can you use the Holy Spirit to scare demons away from your room?

How is the Holy Spirit related to Jesus?

How can the Holy Spirit be with you all the time?

Angels:

Song: "Rescue" by Lauren Daigle

Video: "Angels and Cherubim" from The Bible Project*

VIdeo: "Elohim" from The Bible Project*

Questions:

Have you ever seen an angel? Do you want to see an angel?

Do angels have wings?

What can you do to ask angels to protect you? How can you use them to fight the Enemy?

Prayer:

Song: "What a Beautiful Name" by Hillsong

Book: *Moving Mountains* by John Eldgredge*

Questions:

Do you like praying? Why or why not?

Do you like talking to Jesus?

Are you excited to start learning God's voice? Maybe you can ask him to speak to you right now.

The Bible:
Song: "Thy Word" by Amy Grant
Movie: *What's in the Bible with Buck Denver* from Phil Vischar

Questions:
What is your favorite Bible story? How does it talk about Jesus?
What does it mean that the bible is a "light unto my feet"?
What's something you can do to remember to read God's Word every day?

Growing and Persisting:
Song: "Rest on Us" by Maverick City Music
Book: *The Bondage Breaker* by Neil T. Anderson*
Book: *In the Desert with Jesus* by Mark Shockley*

Questions:
What would it take for you to pray seven times about one thing like Elijah did?
What does it mean to persist? How is that different from being stubborn?
We don't have to work and work for Jesus to love us and help us; he already loves you more than you can know. So, how can you work to be more like Jesus without making it all about you?

Your Heart:
Song: "Holiness" by Sonicflood
Song: "Have My Heart" by Maverick City Music
Book: *You Are Mine* and *You are Special* by Max Lucado
Book: *Captivating* by John and Stasi Eldredge*
Book: *Wild at Heart* by John Eldredge*
Movie: *The Heart of Man*, 2017*
Video: "Heart" from The Bible Project*

Questions:
What is your reason to sing?
What does it mean that we don't have to wait to start living in forever?
Are you glad your heart and soul get to live longer than your earthly body? Do you think you'll get a new body?

Joint Heirs:
Song: "The Family of God" by Bill Gaither

Questions:
Have you ever wanted to be royalty? What will you do differently now that you know you are royalty?
If God is King over everything, how can you be a king or queen, too?
What do you think your throne will look like when you sit by Jesus?

One with Jesus:
Song: "I Don't Need Anything But You" from Annie
Song: "He is Here" by Bill Gaither

Questions:
Do you ever feel empty? Like something is missing? What do you think is missing?
What do you think it will look like to be one with Jesus?
Do you think you'll like it? Being one with your creator?

The Coming Kingdom:
Song: "The King is Coming" by Bill Gaither
Song: "We Shall Behold Him" by Sandi Patty
Song: "Goodbye, World, Goodbye" by W.J.J.M. Radio Gospel Quartet
Book: *All Things New* by John Eldredge*
Podcast: "Expecting the Wonderful" from Wild at Heart Ministries* https://wildatheart.org/rhplay/podcast/expecting-wonderful

Questions:
What's something you're really looking forward to in the New Perfect Place?
What is something you've lost and really want to see again? Do you think it will be in the New Perfect Place?
What do you think it will be like to have a perfect body?
Do you think God will be as excited to see you as you are to see him in his New Perfect Place?

Acknowledgements

A very special thank you to everyone who helped me make this possible. I couldn't have done it without you. You all played a special role and I'm forever grateful to you. Mark Shockley (publishing mentor), Kelly French (grammar editor), Tony French (content editor), Andy Gibbons (content editor), Emily Speake (illustrations and art design), Windha Sukmanindya (Fighting the Great Battle illustration), Winna (The Hope of Jesus illustration), Michel Jamison (section reader), Lanna French (section editor), Erin Pietrzak (youth editor), Bridget Carroll (motivational reader), Blaine Eldredge (motivational reader).

Thanks to the kids who inspire me. I'm excited for you to read this book. Jesus is doing great things in your lives. I'm honored to be a part of it.

Thanks to Jesus. He saved my life. He gave me freedom. And he breathed this entire book into being.

Made in the USA
Middletown, DE
27 September 2021